The Ardent Dark

The Ardent Dark

Don Gutteridge

First Edition

Hidden Brook Press
www.HiddenBrookPress.com
writers@HiddenBrookPress.com
EST. 1994

Copyright © 2021 Hidden Brook Press
Copyright © 2021 Don Gutteridge

All rights revert to the author. All rights for book, layout and design remain with Hidden Brook Press. No part of this book may be reproduced except by a reviewer who may quote brief passages in a review. The use of any part of this publication reproduced, transmitted in any form or by any means, electronic, mechanical, photocopied, recorded or otherwise stored in a retrieval system without prior permission in writing from the publisher or a licence from The Canadian Copyright Licensing Agency (Access Copyright). For an Access Copyright licence, visit: www.accesscopyright.ca or call toll free: 1.800-893-5777.

The Ardent Dark
by Don Gutteridge

Cover Design – Richard M. Grove
Layout and Design – Richard M. Grove

Typeset in Garamond
Printed and bound in Canada
Distributed in USA by Ingram,
      in Canada by Hidden Brook Press

Library and Archives Canada Cataloguing in Publication

Title: The ardent dark / Don Gutteridge.
Names: Gutteridge, Don, 1937- author.
Description: Poems.
Identifiers: Canadiana 20210314850 | ISBN 9781989786529 (softcover)
Classification: LCC PS8513.U85 A93 2021 | DDC C811/.54—dc23

In loving memory
for Tom, my soulmate.

Table of Contents

- All the Waters of the World – *p. 1*
- Bardic Star – *p. 2*
- Tincture – *p. 3*
- Illume – *p. 4*
- Saharan – *p. 5*
- Runnels – *p. 6*
- Bugle – *p. 7*
- Moon-Bloom – *p. 8*
- Babe – *p. 9*
- Tousled – *p. 10*
- Cuddle – *p. 11*
- Soldier's Stride; Point Edward 1945 – *p. 12*
- Tallyho: Sarnia Township 1948 – *p. 13*
- School Day: Sarnia Township 1948 – *p. 14*
- At Play: Point Edward 1948 – *p. 15*
- Beach: Canatara 1944 – *p. 16*
- Yard: Point Edward, 1946 – *p. 17*
- Marvellous – *p. 18*
- Reawakened – *p. 19*
- April Rain – *p. 20*
- Seven – *p. 21*
- Recall – *p. 22*
- Brown-Eyed – *p. 23*
- Injustice – *p. 24*
- Dance: Point Edward 1947 – *p. 25*
- Fettle – *p. 26*
- An October Morning – *p. 27*
- Luxuries – *p. 28*
- Plunge – *p. 29*
- Icy – *p. 30*
- Weft – *p. 31*
- Dunes at Canatara – *p. 32*
- Flotsam – *p. 33*
- Wrought – *p. 34*
- Decree – *p. 35*
- Bite – *p. 36*
- Defrocked – *p. 37*
- Ego – *p. 38*
- Blithe – *p. 39*
- God's Dream – *p. 40*
- Velocity – *p. 41*

- Adam's Dream – *p. 42*
- Winsome – *p. 43*
- Benign – *p. 44*
- One Year On – *p. 45*
- Fletched – *p. 46*
- Heathen – *p. 47*
- Grecian Light – *p. 48*
- Roan – *p. 49*
- When First I Set About – *p. 50*
- Bardic Dark – *p. 51*
- Hummingbird Summer – *p. 52*
- I Never Hear – *p. 53*
- Portents and Parables – *p. 54*
- A Strut in the Step – *p. 55*
- Stroll – *p. 56*
- Toddlers – *p.57*
- Homage: John B. Lee – *p.58*
- Such Fecundity – *p. 59*
- Hummed – *p. 60*
- Flow – *p. 61*
- Skimmers – *p. 62*
- Sweet – *p. 63*
- Gist – *p. 64*
- In the Clover – *p. 65*
- Blunt – *p. 66*
- Bonded in the Bone – *p. 67*
- Devisng – *p. 68*
- Tickle – *p. 69*
- Swelter – *p. 70*
- Storied – *p. 71*
- Afterthought – *p. 72*
- Midnight on Huron – *p. 73*
- Luscious – *p. 74*
- Tickle – *p. 75*
- Jewelled Embrace – *p. 76*
- Embrace – *p. 77*
- Pilgrim – *p. 78*

Author Bio – *p. 81*

All the Waters of the World

As we circumnavigate our village
and pause in the lee of the Lake
to watch the strumpet sun
subside in pied profusion,
I do not take Grandfather's
hand, but sense his presence
in each of our martial strides,
and when First Bush
looms with its shudder of shadow
and leaves unlicked by light
and adders curled like asps
in the toxic grass, something
like fear flickers inside
until those faithful
fingers lean low,
find mine and furl,
and I knew then that blood
is thicker than all the waters
of the world, and love, once
budded, abides.

Bardic Star

When the moon swoons beneath
First Bush, the sun
resumes its hold on the horizon,
flooding the foliage with lickerish
light that breeds in the leaves,
and gilds the grass, where an adder
seesaws on the buff
of his belly and flicks his tongue
like a wanton baton, and robins,
unhobbled in the heat,
dream of procreation
and perilous passage, and bees,
freed from their honeyed hives,
nosh on nectar, and an upstart
breeze brushes the greenery
lustrous, and into this
improvised Paradise
I arrive, like Adam, guesting
in Eden, my head, puffed
with poems and possibility,
looking for words to teem
and stun – and glow like a bardic
star.

Tincture

The summer sun sizzles
above First Bush
and floods its leafage with libidinous
light, stirring in birds
the urge to duplicate
and teasing bees to tantrum
in their honeyed buzz, and an adder
grooves in the grass like a soft
assassin, and all things
green and cousined droop
in the hectic heat, and I too
arrive, like a bard to his bar-
mitzvah, a-burst with the possibility
of poetry and its dithyrambic
dither, and I dip my nib
into ink's tincture, and drink.

Illume

Under Mara's lamp
and the moon's illume, the girls
gather in a gaggle of giggles,
too shy to let
their smiles glide, but chuffed
enough to put a wag
on their tail, while the boys posture
and preen in the laggard light
and wait for something big
to engender in their genes.

Saharan

On Canatara's Saharan sands
I spent the best days
of my boyhood, loitering
like some Adam awol
in Eden, bedazed by the green
scenery, and we built castles
like budding architects
and waited for the surf to lick
them liquid, and when the afternoon
softened around us, we tested
the stilled chill of the water
with the torsion of our toes and let
our bodies be embraced by the lake's
blue brilliance, caring not
that something in the blood rebelled,
felt the alien urge
of being bruised buoyant,
and what relief to sprawl
face first upon
the blistered bevel of a dune
and have our bones warmed
like sun-brushed moons.

Runnels

O how I loved Canatara
and the Lake that lipped it
and the way my body bloomed
in its billowing chill, and I plunged
like a porpoise with a purpose
into its underwater runnels
and rills and let the current
take me where it will, like a
moon-tugged tide
or the indrawn breath of a bride's
surprise, and how wee
we felt – un-at-ease
in such a sea-sized
whim of the world, but pleased
enough to be here at the rim
of the home-horizon – growing
gills.

Bugle

Long ago, when the Earth
had too many moons,
the Attawandaron came
to Canatara to take
the waters, gather clams
and worship their disembodied
gods and when, eons on,
I swam the day away
in my Lake's billowing blue,
I thought I could hear the chime
of their chanting above the
lonesome bugle of a loon.

Moon-Bloom

These dunes at Canatara
are older than Adam's glide
into Eden or Eve's apostasy,
having harvested the heat
of a hundred-thousand suns,
and when I lay my body's
length upon their bevelled
beauty, the warmth they've stored
glows in my slow bones,
and I feel the strength of Earth's
girth and the moon-bloom
of its centuries.

Babe

I wish I'd been more than a babe
when the Babe was in his prime:
the heft of that hickory stick
un-rounding a leathered ball
and setting it a-sail, unaided,
to the right-field choir,
cheering its satisfying swoon,
and when he circled the bases
in those old, flawed films,
I loved the slope of his lope
and the way he tipped his cap
to the crowd when he planted a foot
on the plate, as a gentleman might
his lady, and I think that quest
for perfection was akin to the Bard's
passionate pursuit of pentameters
or an assassin's pristine eye.

Tousled

My grandfather in his Saturday
morning workshop,
me: just high enough
to have my hair tousled,
my tyke's eye
never off those calloused
calming fingers, supple
on the lathe's bright dials,
a slim ribbon of steel
peeling away, an infant's
first curls. and later on,
guiding a lozenge of oak-
grained wood smoothly
through the bandsaw's bitter
buzz, and I felt the smile
of his satisfaction all the way
down to my tousled crown.

Cuddle

It's only a flap of flesh
where the thighs collide, but O
what pleasures it provides
when lovers beatify their bodies
and let their lusts seek
solace in the other's trust,
when desire finds a home
in the furious fire of fusion,
and in the baffled aftermath
of their abrupt uncoupling,
they move to salve and satisfy,
and, for good measure,
cuddle.

Soldier's Stride; Point Edward 1945

For my grandfather in memoriam

Me: half-a-step
behind his soldier's stride,
the map of our village afloat
in his head, we come to the
Slip where sailboats doze
in their own reflection,
waiting for wind to feather them
free, First Bush: shunned
shade, robins hobnobbing
aloft, honey-bees
at home in their nectar-
thriving hive, a garter
snake weaving grooves
in the grass; I talk a-mile-
a-minute into his stoic
smile until the Lake
looms blue in the distance,
its calming façade unflawed,
and we stand side by side,
humbled by the heft of the horizon,
linked in love and awe.

Tallyho: Sarnia Township 1948

The big sled, once
slung with a season's corn,
glides along the winter-
slick country road
behind a pair of Clydes,
siblings at birth,
above: a black bowl
of sky, embossed with stars
and a one-eyed moon
exuding lunar light,
and we are packed,
boys and girls astride
in huddled heaps, our body-
heat a second breath,
no need for gendered
jousting, here on a
celibate curve of the universe
where all flesh is flotsam.

School Day: Sarnia Township 1948

Morning in September,
the trek to school,
dust-puffs where our feet
fling, water welling
in the ditches, a tickle
of sound, on the fringes
goldenrod gleams, shaggy,
wind-shook, our lunch
pails swing with a
shrivelled squeak, girls
on their own side, winsome
and wary, bows in the
halo of their hair, winking,
skirts demure where the
knees knot, boys
boasting, scuffing stones
astray, too brave
to blush, somewhere
a heifer howls, pregnant
with pain, and there
where the schoolhouse
stands immaculate in its
pasture, the big-horned
bull bellows.

At Play: Point Edward 1948

Night settles down
in soft surrender along
our stretch of the street,
aloft, stars define
the architecture of the dark,
the moon eludes a tug
of the tide, its glow giving
shape to shadows that seep
sideways, under, shudder
in the blood, boys and girls
at play where Mara's lamp
lingers light, gendered
bodies in summer's swelter
sweating sex, running
rogue from the thing
that breathes below the breath
towards the Bogeyman,
dancing with Death.

Beach: Canatara 1944

Me just seven, my hand
in his, loving to be led,
a sifting of sand beneath
my feet, free to feel,
a sweep of beach from rim
to rim, a whisper of waves
before they bring their blue
to bear, my eyes a-brim
with vistas, my heart
its own horizon, here
where a world begins
and ends, the day now
deepening towards dark,
a wind nipping
from the lee of the lake,
my fingers furled
in Grandfather's grip.

Yard: Point Edward, 1946

Facing West, the lilac
hedge, lit with lavender,
on the North, sprays of spruce,
bridal bouquets, tiger
lilies and wild iris
to greet the sun good
morning, bees a-doze
nearby, drunk on honey,
the back-forty: hillocked,
a slope to tumble or whee,
southward the wince of privet,
a failed fence, the gate
a relic I rode like a
whirl-i-gig, a sidewalk,
sizzling in summer – the yard:
big enough for my becoming.

Marvellous

In Sunday School we were told
that Jesus glided on Galilee,
fed the multitude with luscious
loaves and fishes, leaned on
Lazarus to hazard resurrection,
confined the blind to sempiternal
seeing, gave paralytics
their legs again, unpalsied
the palsied, and rolled his tomb's
stone away and soared
into Heaven with a levitating
glory, and these were the stories
that stirred and amazed when we
were still at ease with the marvelling
of miracles,.

Reawakened

I was breast-fed on Bible
stories: like Adam and Eve
undressed in Eden
and foraging for figs, or Moses
bundled in a basket and scissoring
seas, or Joshua with his plump
trumpet, jousting in Jericho,
or Daniel dozing off
in the lion's lair, or Shadrach
and his chums toasting their toes,
or Elijah and his incendiary ascension,
or Delilah's surreptitious snip,
or Samson frazzled in Gaza,
or Goliath imperilled by a pebble,
or Zachariah out on a limb
for his Lord, or Job goaded
aghast by his God, and then
there was Jesus, pinioned
on Golgotha like a mummified
moth, only to rise again,
ski with ease on Galilee
and reawaken the World.

April Rain

It was one of those early
April rains that whisper
in the grass and breathe with listless
mists on tulip blooms
just debouched from their bulbs,
and tickle the nipples of new-
born shoots: a time
of bud-thrust and furious
unfurling, and all things
a-green, lusting for light,
and poets dreaming in dactyls
and lambent iambics with fresh
infusions from the Muse,
and I moved into this
magical morn like Puck
on a hobgoblin high,
or a bacchanalian bard,
drunk on rhyme, who plucked
a Parnassian pen and wrote
himself alive..

Seven

That night when the fever
raged, I felt my seven-year
bones moult and heard
the nurse's voice nearby:
"the morning will tell,"
and something tugged me
back from an abyss and,
pumped full of sulfa
drugs and plasma, I lived
to see another dawn
and lie abed for seven
months, waiting for the valves
of my heart to heal, with thousands
of hours to harvest stories
of rabble-rousing heroes
and happy endings.

Recall

I tried to remember that first
time when, for a wondrous
while, I ambled in iambic
and rhymes arrived for the right
reason and poems flowed
like honey seasoned in the hive,
but those moments struck
but once, livid with light
in the harlequin dark, embered
then, and died.

Brown-Eyed

When Nancy Mara embraced me
in her brown-eyed glance,
I felt some virgin
urge in the grip of my groin,
while the better half of my heart
waas thinking "romance."

Injustice

When I stroked the ball far
afield, and in my youthful
exuberance, tossed my bat
aside, I glided around
the bases, unaware
that I'd struck my dog, Moochie,
and my Dad, nearby, accused me
of hurting my best friend,
marched me home and spanked me
for the first and only time,
and I didn't know which
was worse: the spanking
or the injustice.

Dance: Point Edward 1947

A sidewalk, where the verandah
last sagged, summertime
sizzle on the sultry cement,
a hopscotch grid
chalked between granny cracks,
a Mercatur map for our
hop-to-hop, the girls
tossing first,
their long-legged leaping
and splayed arrivals
arouse something
unintended, furtive,
feral, but when they win
(again), the boys cheer
like cherubs begging for one
more immaculate dance.

Fettle

The girls are doing cartwheels
on grandfather's lawn,
happily head-over-heels,
while the boys, between oohs
and aahs. watch for the first
sign of too much thigh
or the wee wink of a crotch,
but settle for girls in fine
fettle and polite applause.

An October Morning
Guelph, Ontario, 1960

It was a bright October morning
when I stood curbside
to watch you roll up
in your silver Beetle, the wind
making music in your cinnamon
tresses, your lemon frock
a-light, and you debouched
like Cleopatra undisturbed
from her barge and threw me
a smile that left my heart
happily hectic.

Luxuries

O the buxom girls of the Point!
bend their bevelled, long-
legged bodies upon the
sun-strummed sands
of Canatara, and the boys,
loitering a-near, in cahoots
with the Venusian moon,
and wondering aloud what
luxuries lay under
those skin-slim
one-piece suits,
and whether or not they would be
among the anointed.

Plunge

What a joy it was
to plunge our boyhood bodies
into Huron's whale-wide
waves and feel out bones
float and our blood race
in runnels to the lungs,
and we shouldered two abreast
into the buoyancy of breakers
that flung us aside like flotsam
and in the simple silence
of underwater eddies and rills,
we could hear heartbeats that might
have been our own and throbs
of thought too new
to be known and the faint
faraway shoaling of the ocean,
and we held our breath like belugas-
on-bail and, like sea-going
gods, grew gills.

Icy

For Bobby Cooper

Coop and I afloat
in Huron's icy blue
that shrivels our shrapnel,
renders our bones remote,
and sets our stiffened stalks
a-bobbing, and later on
in the bathhouse, we compare
shy erections, happy
to feel something other
than our hearts, throb.

Weft

And me almost eleven,
playing host on Grand-
mother's porch: reading
aloud my maiden effort
to a captive audience of three,
and I wooed them with the weft
and weave of my words, but when
I paused for applause, the silence
deafened me.

Dunes at Canatara

These dunes, older
than Methuselah's dam,
lie adrift in their own sleep,
crowned with sea-grasses
that weep in the on-shore
breeze like the wind-ruffled
whiskers of an aging saint,
and when as a boy I coveted
every inch of these summering
hummocks and lay bare-
bodied upon their hoarded
heat, I thought I could feel
the centuries flinch..

Flotsam

My poems are born out of a
blood-and-bone blooming,
the brevity of our brief belonging
and the grit that whittles words
to catch a rhythm-on-the-run
or unlock the mystery of metaphor
and I toss my verses into the
flotsam of the Universe, where they
may sing long enough to be
subsumed by song.

Wrought

For Katie and Rebecca

My girls are the daughters of Eve,
who gave up Paradise
to nibble at the Knowing Tree
and let her body bloom
anew in a world where amity
soothes and satisfies, and suffering
makes us wise, and beauty
finds a home in a lover's
eyes, and words, wrought
out of patience and pain,
unfurl..

Decree

In the immaculate pastures of Paradise,
begonias bloomed without a
budding, and Adam and Eve,
gendered by decree, wondered
aloud beneath the Knowing
Tree, why they lacked
the zest for sex when he
admired the bevelling
of her breast and she, his manly
studding.

Bite

Following Eve's spiteful
bite and Adam's ensuing
chew, *she* basked in the bloom
of her breasts while *he* checked
the status of his apparatus.

Defrocked

O Marybelle Cooper!
still in the unplucked
bloom of your girlhood
(all hummocks and hollyhocks),
and when you stooped to toss me
a wry smile with the silk
of summer in it, I was struck
numb by your blue-eyed
beauty, and made room
in my heathen heart for thoughts
that might have got a god
defrocked.

Ego

When God said "I am
what I am," He didn't have Adam
or his paramour in mind with their need
to gnaw at the Knowing Tree,
to undapple the apple:
happy to forfeit Eden
and the glitter of innocence to nurture
a newly-minted ego
or be enthralled by the throb
of thought or the illicit itch
of sex or the joy, near
or far, in saying simply,
"We are!"

Blithe

For Katie and Rebecca

O my granddaughters!
Still in the budded bloom
of girlhood and all your lithe
loveliness, and I'd like to see you,
here and far into the new
century, groomed for greatness,
star-endued, blithe
in spirit, and I would call down
the angels from their lofty above
to keep you safe in their harbouring
arms, and when it's time,
sing your souls to sleep.

God's Dream

In God's dream of Eden,
flowers would arrive enbloomed
and sparrows sing like sopranos
and bees stay honeyed
in their hives and grasses need
no grooming, and some
semblance of Himself, puffed
out of dust, to enjoy the serene
scenery and welcome Eve
like a dimpled impresario,
and all was well until she
grew jittery under the
Knowing Tree, and stunning
was the news from Paradise
and bitter its bite.

Velocity

My callow curiosity
was at once aroused, when Rory,
our rooster with his blood-budded
cockade, loosed in the pen
with the pullets, strode to the nearest
damsel and, boosting above
her bent behind, rocked
and rode her with eye-popping
panache and feather-furious
velocity.

Adam's Dream

The grass on Grandfather's lawn
was as green as Adam's dream
of Eden and lilacs on the hedges
were licked livid by light
and leaves on the twinned maples
were embossed by the breeze and a robin,
bachelored in his shadow, with a song
throbbing in his throat, and I reconnoitred
my domain like a starved bard
in search of words to wield
the world anew, at ease
here, where love-and-loss
were yet to be born,
and I would loiter at the edge
of everything vivid and find
some inward glimpse
deemed indelible by the dawn.

Winsome

When Eve arrived in the
dappled demesnes of Eden
with her winsome smile, Adam
was instantly smitten, but after
a while, he wished her nudity
annulled, and the apple unbitten.

Benign

When the Lord I didn't believe in,
stepped aside and let you die,
I looked for someone else
to curse other than a universe
that cares naught for the gamut
of our grieving, but I trust your soul
has settled somewhere benign,
softened by some god's
coddling.

One Year On

For Tom in loving memory

All the willows in Gibbon's*
are weeping, their languid leaves
a-droop like elongated tears,
and the meadow grasses are grieving
your rash passing, and the
hundred-year oak,
tethered to the Earth's girth,
has grown another ring
to mark this melancholy
memorial, and I prized your life
above my own, and rue
the day you waved goodbye
and woke in Heaven.

Gibbon's Park, London, Ontario

Fletched

I was just eleven when the Muse
paid a visit to the meadow
of my mind and syllables too
new to be known
danced iambic there
and my quill flowed with a will
of its own into couplets
uncorrupted by rhyme,
and I became a fledgling
balladeer grazing the grass
of Parnassus, and I lusted after
the ruthless truth of poems
and their paralingual feats,
and I longed to write one
that glowed like a Keatsian ode.

Heathen

For Anne in loving memory

I'd like to make love
like a heathen breeding blasphemy
in the face of God's dour
glower, and celebrate the tender
blending of our bodies, and hope
our love lasts as long as
there's a sun to stun
the world awake.

Grecian Light

Everything green and growing,
petalled or not, withers,
away or rots at the root,
and all things alive
and uncorrupted are subject to
the slow implosion of decay,
and so it is, we turn
hither and thither for words
aright to embalm such
bruised beauty and, like Keats
on his lyrical lute, make it
glow like an urn in Grecian
light.

Roan

Grace Leckie's roan,
ripe for rut, struts
into the bay's stall,
and while the boys bray
and the girls snigger, the big
stallion mounts the mare
and pulls the trigger, and we
are all in awe of such
a loveless clutch, such
a rude infusion in such
a bruising embrace.

When First I Set About

When first I set about
to venture verse, it issued
from some fissure in the blood,
a thought-not-yet-wrought,
girdled in words, a feeling
too raw to be believed,
caught in the mesh of a metaphor,
or a notion needing room
to breathe in the parameters
of a poem, and in our greed
to master meaning, we risk
oblivion, and bleed.

Bardic Dark

My poems explode from a
breech in the bone, ballad
or ode, they teeth on marrow,
and something inside me
too deep to deny
warps them willing into the
world, and they are sprung
intact from some bardic
dark, and each iambic
utterance thins my blood
a little more and harrows
the home-zone, where love
still buds, and abides.

Hummingbird Summer

It must be a hummingbird summer
because bees in their numberless
buzzing are brushing the bluebell
blooms with their lush bellies,
and roses on the arch of their arbour
sweeten in the sun, and in the field
beyond my window, once
fallow, winter wheat
thickens and sags, and redwings
nearby whistle a two-
note tune and their country
cousins sparrow the air
with their flocked fluttering,
and along the bone-white
side-road ragweed
ripens among the bull
thistle, and I dream of Keats
and his lonely odes: of nightingales
and Grecian crockery and Autumn's
mistfulness, uttering blood
to abide, and etch his poems
perpetual.

I Never Hear

I never hear a robin
sing the morning in
with his syllabled song and its
melodious ease without
a thought of Tom grieving
in his grave the loss of his days'
allotment, and all the leaves
on all the trees and the breeze
cleaving them are weeping
green in their bereavement
and deworms a-bloat in their ooze
inch upward to see
such suffering and hear
a robin with a song broken
in its throat.

Portents and Parables

I teethed on Bible stories,
plots and portents and parables:
of Adam and Eve naughtily
nude in their garnished garden,
of Noah trawling the high
sea with the world's menagerie,
of diffident David whose slung
sling toppled a titan,
of Joshua who summoned a trumpet
and jettisoned Jericho, of Job,
parrying plagues and jousting
with Jehovah, of Delilah
who lopped her lover's locks
and watched him undazzle
on Gaza, of Daniel in his den
with lions that purred like jittery
kittens, of Shadrack and his pals
dallying in the heathen heat,
of Zacharias trembling
in his tree for a look at his Lord,
and then there was Jesus, gliding
on Galilee or gored on Golgotha
to save the souls of sinners
like me and let me stutter
over such stories and hear them
breed in my dreams.

A Strut in the Step

For Sandy and that summer

There was a strut in my step
and a smirk in my smile as we
ambled the boulevards of our summer-
time town, like wannabe
lovers, your hand hushed
in mine, your hair a hovering
halo, your lips petals
dipped in wine, and I felt
like a punter with a royal flush
who could suddenly tell north
from south and wouldn't let butter
melt in his mouth.

Stroll
With a nod to Keats

When I have fears that I
may cease to be - blood
and-bone-and-body born,
I take a stroll through the
meadows of my mind, where poems
still grow hither
and yon like petalled posies,
unwithered in the sun,
and soothed by their syllabled song,
I read myself alive
and easy for another day's
dawning.

Toddlers
For Joe Organ

You and Tom were just
toddlers, and even though
you were quick of limb
and seldom still long enough
to reload, and Tom was slow
in his bones, you forgave each
other your niggling oddities
and forged a fast friendship
that survived childhood tiffs,
adolescent angst and careers
that careened on ever-widening
roads, and if it were possible
for brother-love to abide
beyond the grave and its might,
yours would gleam like a lover's
grin, blindsided by light.

Homage: John B. Lee

I came late to your lissome
lyrics, that immaculate clamour
of sound and sense, the way
you tossed a lucid noose
over all things nude
in Nature and found a lexicon
suited to the fraught frantics
of our sexual awakening, words
to put the pith in pudendum
or the grr in groin, and a language
to limn your link to the land,
to the holies of the home ground,
to field and fallow, where a lad
could wander lonely and dream
in dactyls of the pristine passion
of poetry, or fancy a future
of love and laurels.

Such Fecundity

I've often wondered if Adam,
that gelded male, noticed
the birds and the bees, or that
the latter buzzed from bloom
to bloated bloom, scattering
pollen upon their tongues'
tumescence, or how the buds
teeming in the trees nudged
sunward to lick the licorice
of the light, or how the Fruit
Forbidden hung plump,
hoping that some hunger
would tickle temptation and pluck it,
or that the anatomy of Eve
had more curves and their cousins
and succulent symmetries,
or that these and such fecundity
would tarnish the dream of Eden.

Hummed

For Tom in loving memory

They say that somewhere
in the star-strummed Universe
there exists a soul so like
to our own, we could be twinned
in a far firmament,
but I did not have to travel
further than the blue bowl
of the sky to find you there
under it, and we hoed same
row for thirty-five
years, finned and feathered
together, and when we lost you,
my heart hemorrhaged
and my soul, severed asunder,
was set adrift like a rudderless
moon, and I was seized
by a rage that seethed inside
like vehement bees hummed
in their hive.

Flow

We learn to love our body
bit by inching bit,
for we are born to an alien
skin, our mind hovering
somewhere above the ballast
of our bones, wondering when
our limbs will find their rhythm
or a tongue teach itself
to sing in syllables or fingers
tempt a tender tune
from an iimmelodious fiddle,
but sometime before
we grow unwise
in our brief bodily abode,
mind and matter meld,
and Van Goghs and Michelangelos
flow.

Skimmers

Grandpa and I on Canatara's
crystalline beach on a July
morning sweetened by sun
and a breeze freshening on our cheeks,
Grandpa watching me skip
saucer-sized skimmers
across the curled crests
of inrushing waves, and counting
the ounce in my bunces like a
brigadier behooving his troop,
and we stood there, side
by side, gazing out
at the soft throbbing of our Lake
and the bevelled blue above,
happily hobbled by love.

Sweet

For Sandy Grocott Gamble

When we waltzed as a taut
twosome, hand in hand,
that lissome summer long
ago, I felt like a peacock
with his feathers fully fanned,
and even though it wasn't
quite love, after all
is said and done you were the
first girl to soothe
my smile with yours and let
it sweeten in the sun.

Gist

In my one-room country
school, where the heat hummed
from the furnace a floor below
and hung hovering above us,
I could, while Miss Nelson
appraised the recitative
of her first-grade readers,
find time to ponder
the snowflakes whispering
on the big-windows and their wintering
light, and daydream
the doldrums away, or wait
for the gist of a poem's felicity,
and feel the teeming of its words
inside me, like something
too bright to un-be..

In the Clover

When first the clover bloomed
and un-fallowed the field
that lay lustrous in the light
brightening my windowed room,
and honey-bees teased
the tender tips too new
to be believed and,
like swimmers into the swooning
of the waves, we dove into
that green four-leaf
desmesne and rolled and rollicked
until our bones floated,
and we felt like undernourished
nuns, feasting on the sun.

Blunt

My best friend Tommy
invites me inside, and his brother
Glen is seated nearby
stroking a massive erection,
and I look in every direction
but one, and wonder how such
a blunt instrument could forage
in a girl's fertile fastness,
and if so, whether or not
she should call for police
protection

Bonded in the Bone

For Tom in loving memory

Your friend Jonathan tells me
I am adored, and certainly
no-one other than you
peregrinated further
into the groomed oeuvre
of my poems or noshed so needily
on the novels I spun to keep
myself unbored,
and I recall now the blue
gaze you unbibbed
from your crib to let me know,
even then, that love alone
would loom luminous in our lives,
for we were bonded in the bone.

Devisng

I remember still the first
syllables to linger loud
upon my lips, and they burst
a-bloom in the precincts of a poem,
where words wielded a will
of their own choosing, and that night,
in the ardent dark, I dreamt
in iambic and felt the nip
of an addiction I would use to devise
improbable rhymes, similes
that sing solo to silence
and immaculate dactyls the Bard
himself might have prized.

Tickle

I was just fourteen when I felt
the first lick of lust
and thumbed my way to a
wild, orgasmic glide
that made my bones molten
and my blood judder, as if
something had come
unbridled in the brunt
of my being and left me
with a tickle that lasted a lifetime.

Swelter
Point Edward, August 1947

I remember the days when the
pavement puckered and the heat-
haze hovered above us like a
sun-muffling mist,
and roses on Mara's Lane,
to spite the swelter, bloomed
ambrosial and the leaves on Gran's
maples drooped in luckless
loops and the last of the lilacs
had long ago lavendered
aloft and all things
still greening wilted
in the sizzle, and we sweated out
the Summer on Canatara
like budding beach-bums
up to our hilts in the cool
jewel of the lake we loved.

Storied

For Anne in loving memory

I'd like to take you
by the hand and walk you
along the sands of Canatara
under a midnight moon
with breakers from our lake foaming
at our feet in fragile fury,
beside dunes older
than Adam's arrival in Eden,
shrouded in shadow or lit
by mellowing light, but you
have gone to your grave where only
the brave with their heathen hearts
abide, and I must stroll
these storied shores
alone, content to let
your soul breathe in my bones.

Afterthought

God confected the Earth
in half a dozen days
and later on, as an after-
thought, added Eden
with a creature like himself
(puffed from dust and *sans*
appendage) to thicken the plot
and tend the flowers and their
perpetual fletching, and brood
about the wayward ways
of birds and bees, and so
it was that Eve arrived,
newly nude and avid
for apples, who woke up
a world away with Adam
and his dangling doodads
and fig-fronds big enough
to cover what their Maker
deemed too toxic
and the tupping couple loved.

Midnight on Huron

Midnight and the moon looms
just above the half-
horizon like a gilded globe,
chaperoned by stars and a lone
planet blooming Venusian,
and the Lake beside me
is dark and deep and its wind-
whetted waves shadow
the shoreline and break
at my feet in foamed explosions,
and roll as far as the distant
dunes, shoaling the jewelled
sand, and if I am to die,
this is where I want my soul
to sleep and my body bide.

Luscious

Shirley joins the parade
on Grandfather's lawn,
brushes the breeze with her
pom-poms, gives
her skirt a girlish twirl
and finishes up with a
high-booted strut
that leaves us light in the head
and luscious in the loins.

Tickle

I was just fourteen when I felt
the first lick of lust
and thumbed my way to a
wild, orgasmic glide
that made my bones molten
and my blood judder, as if
something had come
unbridled in the brunt
of my being and left me
with a tickle that lasted a lifetime.

Jewelled Embrace

For Tom in loving memory

When there is nothing between
the lake and the beach but the sky
with its daytime moon,
coddled by clouds too bright
for our delight, I begin to wonder
if there is a God who hoisted
his Son to Heaven, dreamed
Eden serene and made Man
out of doodads and dust, but then
I remember the cost of being
alive is our demise and loved ones
lost to everything but the slim
mists of memory, and so
it is, I come again
like a pilgrim to this storied
glacial lake to be
baptized anew, to have
the pain of your going purged
in its cool, jewelled embrace.

Embrace

Into the milkweed meadow
where punctured pods release
their silkened seed and butter-
flies buffet on the breeze
and grasshoppers tease
the weeds with their athletic
leaping and larks sing
like indiffident divas and an adder
weaves in indolent ease
and bumblebees connive
in their honeycombed hive
and marsh marigolds supple
in the sun and bulrushes
ruffle scruffy in a wincing
wind, and you show no
compunction in pronouncing
this place "Paradise,"
where we can live in Nature's
bedizened embrace and where
no-one dies before their time.

Pilgrim

When there is nothing between
the lake and the beach but the sky
with its daytime moon,
coddled by clouds too bright
for our delight, I begin to wonder
if there is a God who hoisted
his Son to Heaven, dreamed
Eden serene and made Man
out of doodads and dust, but then
I remember the cost of being
alive is our demise and loved ones
lost to everything but the slim
mists of memory, and so
it is, I come again
like a pilgrim to this storied
glacial lake to be
baptized anew, to have
my bereavement pain purged
in its cool, jewelled embrace.

Don Gutteridge was born in Sarnia and raised in the nearby village of Point Edward. He taught High School English for seven years, later becoming a Professor in the Faculty of Education at Western University, where he is now Professor Emeritus. He is the author of more than seventy books: poetry, fiction and scholarly works in pedagogical theory and practice. He has published twenty-two novels, including the twelve-volume Marc Edwards mystery series, and forty books of poetry, one of which, Coppermine, was short-listed for the 1973 Governor-General's Award. In 1970 he won the UWO President's Medal for the best periodical poem of that year, "Death at Quebec."

Don lives in London, Ontario.

Email address: dongutteridge37@gmail.com.